WHITES ONLY

WHITES ONLY

Chenoa hARTherapy Murray

MOUNTAIN ARBOR
PRESS

Mountain Arbor
Press
Alpharetta, GA

ISBN: 978-1-63183-393-9 - Paperback
eISBN: 978-1-63183-394-6 - ePub
eISBN: 978-1-63183-395-3 - Mobi

10 9 8 7 6 5 4 3 2   1 1 1 5 1 8

Printed in the United States of America

∞This paper meets the requirements of ANSI/NISO Z39.48-1992 (Permanence of Paper)

Cover photo by Austin Ashby
Artwork by Tony Sierra

To Mother, Daddy, Cinnamon Denise and Gogo

ACKNOWLEDGMENTS

I don't even know why I am even attempting to thank God because no words will be sufficient enough. *Thank you, Jesus!* My gratitude for my immediate and extended family is endless. From my family in America, particularly in Atlanta, Georgia, I say 'thank you'. To my Navajo and Pascua Yaqui friends, my loved ones in South Africa, my companions in Mexico, Costa Rica and China your support has been tremendous.

I will do my best to thank everyone, even though that is a very dangerous feat. Please know that I love you all! Thank you: Mother (the original QUEEN), Daddy (come on, MANE!), Cinnamon Denise (Your #1 fan), Gogo (ngiyakuthanda kakhulu), ALL of my aunties and uncles (biological or otherwise), Kristyn Shaw and Mary Brooks, Mea (I will never fear the red pen!), Darmea (sang, chile!), Taneisha (Neeeeish!), Adam (Bursharoni!), Mrs. Leah (my lovely lady libra sistuh!), Maneka (Love you forever and ever Amen), Carlos (WOZAAA!), Damien (this is just the beginning for us), Stan the Man (you already know), Keith (my brutha, good looking out!), Chelsea (hey, QUEEN!), Mahalia (Love you, Sweet Pea!), Siphelele (business man with a plan), Njabulo (you are so sweet!), Thandolwethu (best hostess!), Jay Mak (focused and driven), Liyanda (you are the best bodyguard), Creatives 2 Creatives of Emnambithi (bafowethu bami), Mmanoko Poetry Queen Kgathi (love you, sisi!), Snegugu and Ma Msibi (we will see you again, Angel), Hlengiwe, Sbu,

Sindi, Mininhle, Oluwande, Filbert, Dr. Naeema Olatunji (WHAT BALANCE?? haha), my favorite piano player, Symone Superstar, Angelina Sherie (my beautiful sis!), Bryncia (always remember that LaWasha loves you, LaDrya!), Jane and Cathy (my crew!), Nancy (ngiyabonga umngane wami), Pam (thanks for loving my soul and respecting my culture), Joey (uyisikhoko!), LaToya and Sabrina (what would I have done without ya'll?), Betty (all I can say is....COOKIES!), Kajal (thank you for taking a stranger in), Halalisani, Juliet Henry (you leave me speechless, girlfriend), Mr. Kevin Taylor (my teacher, my friend), Mary Anne and Joy Radebe (Izinkosazane Zami), my Personal Consultant Stephanie (reciprocity and vision boards right?), Divinity Church International, Bishop Frederick Nah, Pastor Karen Nah, Dr. Booker, Mr. Victor Baker, Mr. Sabelo Molefe, Mr. Brooks Buthelezi, Scelukukhanya Home Based Care (thank you for teaching me more than I could have ever taught you) and I Am Free Music Festival, LLC.

How does one say 'thank you' for all of the support? I hope that in between the lines of text, my appreciation is apparent and my 'thank you' is enough.

FOREWORD

In a world where blatant honesty is almost a thing of the past, and raw introspection of self and nation is unheard of in the new millennium, author Chenoa hARTherapy Murray digs deep into the psyche of man, and forces you to examine pass wrongs, the internal struggles of love and more!

In her poetic masterpiece " Whites Only, " she will engross you with transcending love, peace, justice and forgiveness. The thought provoking ideas and questions will change hearts and minds in this revolutionary book of poetry.

I can recall phone conversations Chenoa and I had while she was in the Peace Corps, stationed in South Africa . She mentioned to me a poem she had written called " The Apology," and she started to recite. I was captivated and locked in a moment I shall never forget, with the added bonus days later, the iconic shot of her sitting on a Whites Only bench which is now her book cover! Needless to say, but at that moment she was booked on Visionary Talk Radio! And there my inception of the world of poetry with Chenoa began.

Chenoa speaks to all ages and humanitarians at heart, giving us a new perspective via " Whites Only." The words of this book will penetrate even the hardest of minds and will stand the test of time simply because it speaks truth, it speaks humanity, it speaks love, it speaks power.

Juliet Henry, Host of Visionary Talk Radio

THE ARRIVAL

From me to all of you who watched, I thank you.
From me to all of you who carried me, I thank you.

To all of you that never doubted me and even those who did
For every good intention turned bad decision? It's okay.

Arrival. It's The Arrival.

My prayers were answered anyway.
No longer am I concerned with
the unrealized dreams in the Dreamcatcher's web. I no
longer pay mind.
no longer pay mind. NO LONGER pay mind.

Because today I am here. Sufficient for the Universe and
everything God intended.

It's The Arrival.

*The story of the Dreamcatcher originates from the Great Lakes of
the Ojibway Nation. The circle of life within a spun web catches
the bad dreams while the hole in the center lets the good dreams
float through and down the feathers hanging off the Dreamcatcher
to the sleeper. Tokens can be added onto the Dreamcatcher by the
owner for luck and such. ~Marilyn Tsinajinnie*

VICTORY

Why do they fall? Tears, that is. To remind us we've failed?

Negative. To instruct us that the weight is now over and in its place we exchange our bowed heads for lifted hands of victory.

CRUSH

- *Crush* – (verb) to press between opposing bodies so as to break or injure

- *Crush* – (noun) the intense infatuation for someone

How could something so painful be so desired among men?

Crush.

So much beauty in its sting.

Watch out; poison is often clothed in charm.

FLOW WITH ME

AUTOMATIC THOUGHTS FLOW

i'm going to disappoint them

i'm going to fail

i'm scared to fail

i'm overwhelmed

i can't do this

i don't really want to do this

STOP.

why won't my thoughts
cooperate with me?
what is their problem?
Flow with me for just a
minute here.
I did not ask for this.

But here I am.

so loud, these thoughts of
mine. choppy.

I'd rather flow.
Can you do that, thoughts?
Can you just flow with me?
and stop holding up progress?

What is 'Just'?

Live and die for Justice
Because it's never been about JUST US

Politics. No, Poli*tricks* among us.
Sweetly sing the tunes of "...and the Land of the free, and
the home of the slave-
　　　　I mean, brave, BRAVE, BRAVE!"

You can run but you cannot hide beyond
the wall. Border. Walls. Stretch until the
tippy tops kiss the dusty horizon.

Live and die for Justice
Not for thoughts of JUST US

Yeah your ancestors were slaves. So were Mayan.
If you subscribe to the notion that man has the last word
you're still eating slavery's bitter fruit. But tell someone.
Help someone. Touch somebody.

Instead of worrying about JUST US
Die to live for JUSTICE.

FATE

conscience clear
head on straight
lead Me to
My only fate...Freedom

BETWEEN THE TWO OF US

Forever never felt so long
blowing awry like dust and tumbleweed
I regret to inform yet again with emphasis
your voice makes my ears bleed

The sly stride in your step
I attempt to ignore
how much it upsets me
when you appear at my door

It wasn't always like that
between you and I
at one point without you
I thought I might die

Amazes me so
the enmity betwixt us
for seldom anger grips me
now I'm jailed in its clutch

Side-eye, deep sigh
is how we start conversation
willingness to change?
we've both grown impatient

Dissention and strife
we live our years
no mention of Love
only gossip from peers

Perhaps with time
or when death do us part
can child and mother
mend the wounds in our hearts

PLAYING FAVORITES

pink lemonade, fresh painted toes, soft chocolate kisses
upside down roller coasters, sink with no dirty dishes

favorite things
my favorite things

MIND RECLINE

Relax the reigns. Forget it.
Morality? What is that?
Let it go. Numb.

Everybody loves a winner, maybe that's why nobody loves me.

Relax the reigns and transform your mind.

FOR HIS EYES ONLY

Gripped her shaky, glistening body
traced her slender frame

ever so lightly did he grasp the mahogany
now engulfed by his unsteady hand   the old man.

withered by experience and tested by time,

enjoyed the cool, glossed wood of his walking stick.

EMERGENCY

THIS MAN IS WORKING MY DAMN NERVES

and I'm loving every minute of it

Somebody help me!

sweet bliss engulfs me tenderly
but it hurts; it hurts like hell

I can't have you – not yet.
Love is too young and the heart too tender.
Besides, God must be his number one and He's not.

so WHY IN THE WORLD is he making love to my mind?

no rubbers.

REVELATION

Once is a sign
Twice a confirmation
Thrice will suffice
    my joyous revelation

RESERVATIONS AND BORDERS

Fence you in.

    Keep me safe.

    "You can take the dog out of the reservation, but
you're still
just a dog."

    Shame.

THE APOLOGY

Christianity, Christianity
Oh where, oh where is your Humanity?

So heavenly-minded that you are no earthly good.
But today I understood.
Many have questioned and I have been unable to articulate a
response, until now.

It hurts.

How can you believe in a religion that enslaved your Mothers
exiled your Brothers
robbed your Sisters of their purity
obliterated Father's pride, his dignity?
Masqueraded behind facades of honor and glory, yet showed
their true colors through wealth, stealth, and gluttony.

Christianity, Christianity
Oh where, oh where is your Sanity?

THE AGONY!

Ancestors ripped from their families to slave in mines,
never to see loved ones for months, maybe years at a time.
Born into a system sprinkled with *just enough* education to
labor to death for an ingrate.
Whites who opposed?   Kidnapped and never heard from
again. And THIS?!

THIS all in the name of a
righteous,
Savior?
A righteous, white Savior?
Come to save us from our sins? Our filthy *black* sins?
Please, say it isn't so.

"Christianity"
seems to be
nothing but **DEPRAVITY**
such **CALAMITY**
it's plain to see
its rotting with **PROFANITY**
but that's in terms of US, you see
this humble and perfect **DEITY**
Who **HE IS** to me can
overcome man's **FRAILTY**
He came to be
so you and me
could love and live **ABUNDANTLY**
a **RARITY** hardly spoken
of this God
that I love.

It matters **not** to me
which color his skin reflects the light we see

What matters most is red He bled
and that, THAT is how I am certain of His HUMANITY.

Christianity is hope to me. Terribly misused to control the
free;
This is an <u>Apology</u>!

I do admit, a human error, wroth with endless shame
but it's people and not God who is to blame.

QUEEN

Kissed by celestial glow
The Woman, her stride
Freedom knows no boundaries
and neither do I.

La Reina
El besado por el brillo celestial
La Mujer, su paso
La Libertad no conoce limites
ni yo tampoco.

Koningin
Gesoen deur n hemelse gloei
Die Vrou, met haar stap
Met Vryheid sonder grense
en nog minder Ek.

Inkosazane
Ngokukhanya kwezulu
Owesifazane, isinyathelo sakhe
Inkululeko ayiko imingcele
futhi nami.

You see, it does not matter whether you have evolved through
English,
whether you sway in Spanish,
whether you are excited about Afrikaans
or if your love for IsiZulu is insatiable

My Dear

You are still

Kissed by celestial glow
The Woman, yes, YOU woman,
Your stride
Freedom knows no boundaries
and neither
do you
nor I.

POP QUIZ

And I'm proud to be an American, where at least I know I'm free.

Open gravesite. Massive gravesites. Open vats of human disgrace. Pits of despair.

But still I'm proud to be an American, where at least I know I'm free?
to roam under the siege of oppression. Centuries' old traditions as American as apple pie.

Yes! Better yourself and get all the education you can! But please be sure to be born into the Silver Spoon Family, population one percent.

Yet I'm proud to be an American,
where at least
I know
I'm _____(YOU fill in the blank).

SPIRITBIRD JOURNEY

<u>PART I:</u>
The Fear

Spiritbird soars high and soul free. Airy, take flight.

but not this time.
the worry? gripping.
cease flight altogether.
a new path to reconsider. on shattered wings of anger,
Spiritbird's glide is interrupted. stop abrupt. horizon is too far
for Spiritbird.

Climb! Try!
And rest in forgiveness' nest!

but Spiritbird stays grounded.
paralyzed in imprisonment and trapped by choice, it is here
Spiritbird remains.

fearful.

<u>PART II:</u>
The Surrender

Flying is *not* easy
Lacking strength, determination, or courage is not an option.

Spiritbird knows that, but is
detached at the moment.

The flight is intimidating.
Hesitant and fatigued, Spiritbird lays
down to rest in surrender...for good.

PART III:
The Reminder

Anxious.

Anxious to fly again.

Rise one last time, Spiritbird. above the rest, above the noise.

How will Spiritbird ever appreciate The Arrival
        without first an arduous process?

Life's flight is not only about the destination,
it's about the journey.

Rise within to rise again.

DO YUH THANG

Valerie she made me strong
my Daddy helped me keep laughing on
my Cinnamon said don't worry 'bout dem, girl
do yuh thang and it'll come 'round, come 'round

Just like a fiya come 'round, come 'round

Don't worry 'bout dem, just do yuh thang yeah
do yuh thang, sistuh

either dey'll luv yuh or dey won't

EL TREN DE LA MUERTA (DEATH TRAIN)

History's-A-Knocking

Religious. Strong work ethic. Family-oriented.

Escape from India, 40 of them. Some criminal; others not so.

Broken families, visit the fence for Christmas.

Rape. Mistrust. The silent bell of domestic violence rings sharply and clear.

Detention. Indeed this is a business.

Jail economics, no, people economics. Trans corridor region.

Sacrifice the front line. False claims and fake documents. Swallow this marijuana. Ride with us to your death.

This is border life. La Frontera.

TOGETHER

BABY, if you can hear me, I'm whispering in your ear as you slumber tonight.
Sweet nothings.

This is not about sex, although a beautiful thing it is indeed.
This is much deeper than that.

The nucleus moves in rhythm with the mitochondria
& the moon with the ocean waves
& the time with the season
& the ebb with the flow,
that is how we move together.

We move in life's rhythm today.
Whether pain or pleasure, we're always on the same page, same paragraph.

I love God even more than I thought was humanly possible for creating you. Almost as if Perfection couldn't keep up, it had to take a backseat when you Arrived on the scene of my life.

My heart is full and sure.

UNDERDRESSED

this world has fancy ceilings
a threshing floor
its ladder of success is decorated with promises of a better
tomorrow

and I am underdressed.

3-piece, tailor-made suits fit for the best of them
educated minds traverse this space seeking easier ways and
increased productivity

but My attire is unacceptable.

9 to 5
I tarry not a minute after that
for another deadline, another day, another dollar

still I'm adorned in unvalued garb.

My thoughts speak change,
the system buckles under my stride

how DARE I enter in such useless wear!

Violet scarves for my crowning glory
hair that defies gravity
carrying the cradle of life in my hips

yet they don't want Me.

they want 3-piece, tailor-made suits fit for the best of them
yet in these printed patterns I adore
only fellow Royalty will understand

think it not strange when I enter this world anyway
to take what is rightfully mine and retreat to the Throne Room
from whence I came.
underdressed and late for My next meeting with Destiny.

SEARCHING FOR LIES

"I Love You..."

TIME STOPPED.

I don't even remember breathing.
because in that moment, in *that* moment? I searched for
equivocation. Dubious undertones. I looked for some sort of
ulterior motive, some reason that he would lie and say these
things to me.

but I found none. Not one inkling of doubt was etched on his
lips so when my ears rung of sweet bliss and "I Love You"
tapped ever so gently against my ear drum nothing but
assurance and honesty vibrated through my cochlear, into my
brain, and reverberated within the pit of my longing soul.

THIS was real, HE was real and my mind, body, and soul froze
in a moment in time of which I can never get back. This man,
this damn near perfect man, loves me.

ORDER OUT OF CHAOS

where did I go? my passion wanes and I grow weary.
But falling I shall rise.

Sometimes you must go low in order to go high.

Let the seeing ears live and the hearing eyes stand up.

what to do? what to do?

<u>Whatever is in your heart.</u>

Speak life. And be positive for positivity's sake!

DUH!

Black.
We are taught to tolerate.

The Jews wear that funny little thing on their head. Okay.
That's cool.

Who? Them?
Oh they're Native American so you'll have to excuse their language.
They were here first ya know.

And don't mind the Latinos. Some like to be called Hispanic, not Latino. Please be sensitive to their needs.

Don't bully others! You don't know what they're going through!

You gotta be extra nice to gay people.
They were made that way.

You can't discriminate against women!
Whatever happened to all men are created equal?

You can't call them white. The correct term is Anglo or of European descent. Don't mess it up.

Not all Asians are from China so you can't call them that. Ask them their history. Who they are. That's what they want. Be culturally sensitive. It's only right. Remember to tolerate EVERYthing and EVERYbody.

that is
EVERYthing and EVERYbody
not
like
me.

But don't you drink koolaid? They say.
Of course I do. It's good. But so do a million other people.

But I thought you ate fried chicken.
No shit.   And Italian pasta, Mexican tamales, Indian curry
chicken, Chinese egg rolls and German chocolate, smart ass.

But I just saw you roll your neck.
I only do that to scare you cuz otherwise ya dumb ass won't
listen.

I thought you were gonna hit me!
You keep this shit up and I will. Now pass me the remote.
The game is on.

and no
you CAN'T
touch my hair.

GRAND RETURN

you OUGHT to be AUTHENTIC
you CAN be CONGRUENT
don't CUT CORNERS,
CUT the CHAOS & CALM down with CONGRUENCY

but   HOW?

what if they don't like me?
what if they don't approve?
How can I face them?
I can't
I can't face any of them so I freeze.
freeze up and hide

but now that I'm hidden, what happens now?
         nothing.

EXACTLY.

Emotions high, almost drowning in fear, but the will to live,
and not merely exist,
is too overpowering.

Too AWESOME to *not* be AUTHENTIC
Too COOL to live without CONGRUENCY

                Just give me time. I'll be back.

FREEDOM HUES

never did the green look so forest

when the Black so slave

entered the dark so midnight

when e'er did the soft so grass

bare His Truth so naked

and truth was revealed in a Georgia field the following
sunrise

when the slave so Black

held a head so high

when the jagged switch plundered His Skin.
His Truth.

but never again will the blood run so Red

since so colorless is the escape.

HE SAID HE LOVES ME

I've only been here once before.
But that was one time too many for me.

Am I really lovable? The text mocks me.
Can this be my new reality?

Forget the bells, the whistles can wait

I'm sitting at Love's gate and the doorstep is warm, inviting
me in for a drink. Let's sip.
Indulge in this love together and thirst for it no more.

Quenched.
Succulent flavor of Love's sweet and tender taste is nothing
short of divine.
Oh yes, we share; but do I divulge what I'm yearning inside?

Wait.

I make him wait at Love's gate and yes, the doorstep is
warm, inviting him in for a drink.

LIKE THE WIND

Like the wind
GOD is like the wind
LOVE is like the wind

You can't see it, but you can feel it
And you know it's there because you can witness its effects
everywhere. You're not exactly sure where it comes from or
even where it's going;

But you have no doubt in your mind that it exists.

About the Author

Chenoa hARTherapy Murray is a premier social justice activist specializing in poetry, public speaking, and voice. With much of her work based on the importance of cultural diversity and acknowledgement of the human condition, she uses original ear candy to nourish the hART and soul of audiences worldwide.

Ultimately, it is Chenoa hARTherapy Murray's goal that all who hear her words are reenergized, invigorated, and inspired to give life just one more try. She lives by her own mantra, "No matter what happens, don't die before you enter the grave, live while you are yet living!"

When she is not writing, she can be found eating roti and creating new banana-avocado-essential oil combinations to put in her hair.